~◆~

Shattered Hope:

Infertility

A 30-day
Dust2 Diamond Devotional

Nancy Faltermeier & Kelly Sumner

Sword Sower Publishing

SwordSower Publishing
P.O. Box 98
Eastlake, Colorado 80614
www.swordsowerpublishing.com

SwordSower Logo – Jan Marie Wirth

Cover Design – Nancy Faltermeier

Editor – Juliet Kennedy

Publisher's Note: This is a work of non-fiction, while stories are true, names and locales have been changed to protect identity. Any resemblance to actual people, living or dead, or to businesses, companies, events, or institutions is completely coincidental. Although every precaution has been taken to verify the accuracy of the information contained herein, the author and publisher assume no responsibility for any errors or omissions. No liability is assumed for damages that may result from the use of information contained within.

Book Layout © 2016 BookDesignTemplates.com

Shattered Hope: Infertility/ Nancy Faltermeier & Kelly Sumner. -- 1st ed.
Print Edition ISBN 978-1-945391-02-6
Kindle Edition ISBN 978-1-945391-03-3

Dedication

We dedicate this book to all those who yearn for children. May our efforts bring you solace and comfort through your struggle. We pray your shattered hope will be mended and restored in Him.

Acknowledgments

All our thanks go to Juliet Kennedy, our editor, whose well-placed suggestions made our words sing. We will forever be grateful.

We also acknowledge the input from those who critiqued this work. Thank you. You know who you are.

Contents

~ ◆ ~

Day 1 with Nancy
A Bird's Desire

There are three things that will not be satisfied,
four that will not say, "Enough":
Sheol, (the grave) and
the barren womb,
Earth, that is never satisfied with water,
And fire, that never says, "Enough."
Proverbs 30:15–16

For two decades, my family has kept parakeets as pets. One parakeet, a white and pale-blue female named Blizzy, and her mate, an older male named Snowbell, taught me invaluable lessons about a mother's desire for a baby and facing fears.

One day my daughter left a paper towel on the grate near the bottom of the cage. A week later, Blizzy gleefully had shredded it. As my daughter cleaned the cage, she found a tiny white ball among the shreds. Wondering what it was, she gave the orb a tiny squeeze, and it cracked open. In tears, she brought her discovery to me. Blizzy had laid an egg.

All of the little bird's happiness deflated like a balloon at her loss. There she sat, her little white head sagging below her perch. Confident I'd make her happy, I brought home a nesting box and put it in the cage, even though I didn't want to raise baby parakeets. The lady at the pet store assured me the eggs rarely hatch, unless we had a true pair of birds.

Blizzy was afraid of the nesting box. Snowbell entered and exited it several times, demonstrating the safety of the wooden abode, but Blizzy wasn't convinced. Still desperate to lay eggs, she attempted to pull up the newspaper lining under the cage's grate. She could only manage a tiny mouthful of newsprint and each time thumped the grate. This thumping went on day after day, week after week, month after month. Snowbell perched above her with great patience.

After five months passed, Snowbell couldn't take the noise and nonsense any longer. Screeching loud and long, he gave her a piece of his mind. The thumping stopped. I found Blizzy working on her nest inside the box, and by day's end, she had laid six tiny eggs.

Happy Blizzy sat faithfully on her eggs. A gleeful Snowbell fed his mate. Joy oozed from the cage. And then a tiny hatchling called to its mother. The exuberance of the new parents spilled into the room as they doted on their little offspring.

On the third morning, the cage sat quietly. The infant bird lay still.

I identified with Blizzy after my struggles with infertility. During my quest for a child, I puzzled over the desperate desire to fill my arms. Why couldn't I just go on and be happy childless? I asked the Lord to take the desire away, but He never did. Proverbs 30:16 tells us that the barren womb never says, "Enough." God gave many of us a desire to reproduce. It's the nature of earthly life. We shouldn't think it's something odd. Many of us were created with the natural desire to fulfill God's first command: "Be fruitful and multiply" (Genesis 1:28).

Blizzy also taught me about facing fears. Because she was afraid of the nesting box, she tried another method to build a nest without success. How much easier her life would have been if she'd entered the nesting box earlier. Has the Lord put a nesting box in your life, such as medical treatment or adoption, but your fears hold you back? Have you been trying the same thing over and over again with no success? The Lord understands your dilemmas and wants to show you what to do. Turn your ear to Him.

I thank You, Lord, that You understand what I'm going through. Help me to see the "nesting box" You've provided for me and help me not allow fear to prevent me from entering it.

Where fear reigns progress stalls.

What fears do I have concerning infertility? What fears do I have about adoption?

_____

_____

_____

_____

_____

_____

_____

_____

_____

_____

_____

_____

_____

_____

_____

_____

_____

_____

_____

_____

_____
_____
_____
_____
_____
_____
_____
_____
_____
_____
_____
_____
_____
_____
_____
_____
_____
_____
_____
_____

~ ◆ ~

Day 2 with Nancy
Does It Seem Hopeless?

Now faith is the assurance of things hoped for,
the conviction [evidence] of things not seen.
For by it the men of old gained approval.
Hebrews 11:1–2

H as another monthly cycle come and gone and you find once again you're not pregnant? The Lord knows how desperate we can become for a child and how discouraging infertility can be. Month after month, cycle after cycle, we face disappointment. It's easy to allow our faith to erode and our hope to turn into hopelessness. In these moments, we must be careful to not give in to the assault on our faith and hope.

Abraham is one of the "men of old" that the above scripture talks about. Here is a man who dealt with infertility and believed God, not just for a child, but for an entire nation to come from him. Year after year, the promised child did not come, and Abraham and Sarah grew older. The situation seemed hopeless, but Abraham did not allow his faith to waver or his hope to turn to hopelessness. Instead, he kept his faith and hope in the Lord.

Psalm 146:5 says, "How blessed is he whose help is the God of Jacob, Whose hope is in the Lord his God." Romans 5:5 reminds us that "hope does not disappoint, because the love of God has been poured out within our hearts through the Holy Spirit who was given to us." Hope does not disappoint if our hope is in the Lord.

Abraham endured the same trial of infertility you are facing but kept his faith and hope. In Hebrews 11, he was listed in the Hall of Faith where people from the Bible are mentioned for their strong faith in God. The Lord wants to accomplish more in our lives than just give us children. He wants to develop women and men of faith, and sometimes He uses the trial of infertility to do that.

Let Him use this ordeal to do the work He wants to do in your life.

I need You, Lord. Help me to put my hope in You when I see only failure. Thank You for the work You are doing in my life through this trial and give me the power to keep my faith in you because Your Word tells us that You are faithful.

○✝◆✝○

We are not people who have no hope, if we keep our faith in the Lord.

What thoughts and attitudes can I change to strengthen my faith and hope and to see how God is working wonders in my life?

_____

_____

_____

_____

_____

_____

_____

_____

_____

_____

_____

_____

_____

_____

~◆~

Day 3 with Kelly

Infertility Is Just a Word

The one who guards his mouth preserves his life;
The one who opens wide his lips comes to ruin.
Proverbs 13:3

Infertility is an ugly word. We are embarrassed to admit we deal with it. Words can teach and touch our lives, or they can bring pain and lies. Words are alive, and once spoken, we can't take them back. We must speak truth over our lives and our infertility. Instead of saying, "I'll never have a child," we can speak words of hope and believe that with God all things are possible as seen in Matthew 19:26 (ASV).

Words without truth can be uninformed, opinionated, gossipy, and exaggerative. Words build up or tear down. Infertility doesn't need to be an ugly word proclaimed over our lives, and this word should not define who we are.

The Father created us with a unique destiny. Just like a snowflake or fingerprint, each of us is one of a kind.

Speak truth over your life by speaking scripture, and live your faith in your words.

Lord, guard my tongue that I may only speak truth over others and myself. Create in me a pure heart, and help my words to edify all who hear them.

o✝ ◆ ✝o

Words are a window to our heart.

Even in our infertility, we can use our words to support one another and bring comfort to those in need. What words can I speak over my life now?

_____

_____

_____

_____

_____

_____

_____

_____

_____

_____

_____

_____

_____

_____

_____

_____

_____

_____

~ ◆ ~

Day 4 with Nancy

His Ways Are Not Our Ways

The steps of a man are established by the Lord,
And He delights in his way.
Psalm 37:23

A couple tried for some time to get pregnant, even though pregnancy posed a risk to the woman's life. Then they received an opportunity to adopt a little person boy from a foreign country that took a negative view of children born with physical needs. The wife, who did not want to undergo more fertility treatments, was thrilled with the prospect of becoming a parent through adoption and saving this boy from a hard life.

God opened an unexpected door.

This couple followed the way opened to them and have been blessed. They had no previous knowledge of this little boy, but God knew him and wanted him rescued from a life of orphanages and discrimination. This child's smile and zest for life has brought untold joy and wholeness to this family. There is a reason our ways are not His ways. We often don't know the needs that are out there, and the Lord truly knows best.

Help me, Lord, to be willing to step onto the paths You set before me, even if they aren't the ones I want to take. I believe that Your road leads to a fulfilled life. My dreams for the future may not be the dreams you have for me, but I will trust that You know what's best for me and my family.

○✝◆✝○

I can't go wrong stepping onto the path He sets before me.

What paths has the Lord set before me that I can step onto?

_____
_____
_____
_____
_____
_____
_____
_____
_____
_____
_____
_____
_____
_____
_____
_____
_____
_____
_____
_____
_____

~◆~

Day 5 with Nancy

Mother's Day

Cast your burden upon the Lord and He will sustain you;
He will never allow the righteous to be shaken.
Psalm 55:22

Back when I struggled to get pregnant, our church had the tradition on Mother's Day of calling all mothers to the front, praying for them, and giving them a gift. This was the hardest day of the year for me. It rubbed salt in the wounds of my empty arms. Was it God's intention to expose my childlessness to the world?

One Mother's Day during the church service, tears fell uncontrollably. After that embarrassing occurrence, I felt a release from the Lord from attending church on Mother's Day. It eliminated unnecessary pain, and I knew He understood my grief.

If you attend church every Sunday and struggle the way I did, you may want to consider celebrating the Lord differently on Mother's Day. Some may feel uncomfortable with this suggestion, but I am convinced the Lord receives no pleasure in our suffering.

When God answered our prayers and gave us a child, we again participate in the Mother's Day service, with joy in our hearts, and we remember the miracle He has done for us.

Thank you, Lord, that you are not a hard task master, but a Father that knows our pain and struggles. Help me to know You for who You really are and not to believe the lies of the enemy, who would paint You as a vindictive God.

∘✝◆✝∘

The loving God is a lover of my soul.

What do I believe about the Lord that isn't true?

_____

_____

_____

_____

_____

_____

_____

_____

_____

_____

_____

_____

_____

_____

_____

_____

_____

_____

_____

_____

_____

_____

~ ◆ ~

Day 6 with Kelly
Is My Body Broken?

The Lord is near to the brokenhearted
And saves those who are crushed in spirit.
Many are the afflictions of the righteous,
But the Lord delivers him out of them all.
Psalm 34:18–19

One of the issues that made getting pregnant difficult for me was irregular menstrual cycles. As women, we often believe we have one job to do: have children. When we can't do that, we feel we are broken.

Do not lose heart. We live in a broken world, but we are not broken. If our heart's desire is to have a child, God can open the impossible door. It may not be in the way we expect. Sometimes children come from other mothers, and sometimes when we think all hope is lost and the beast of infertility has broken us, God opens our wombs. Seek the Lord and hang on tight to Him. He is the God of the impossible.

Thank You, Lord, for allowing Your body to be broken for me. By Your stripes, I am healed. Because You were broken, I am not. Help me, Lord, to see myself the way You see me.

○✝◆✝○

Absolutely nothing is impossible with God.

Make a list of things God can't do. There shouldn't be anything on it right? Because, is there anything God can't do? What is my heart's desire?

_____

_____

_____

_____

_____

_____

_____

_____

_____

_____

_____

_____

_____

_____

_____

_____

_____

_____

_____

_____

Day 7 with Nancy

Limiting The Goal

Commit your works to the Lord,
And your plans will be established.
Proverbs 16:3

A short one hundred years ago, the only options available to an infertile couple were adoption or remaining childless. Today, medical science provides many more options, but each comes with a price tag. Everyone's situation is different; thus everyone's limits will vary.

Make the Lord the center of your baby quest. Pray, pray, pray for wisdom and guidance.

Consider your financial situation. Do you have insurance to cover the cost of infertility treatments, which can be expensive with no guaranteed results? Remember, the Lord provides for the direction you should go.

Pursue your goal with a plan. Include God in this planning and allow Him to direct you as you and your spouse go forward. Set limits on what kind of infertility treatments you will pursue and which ones you will not. What treatments are pleasing to God? How much money are you willing to spend? How long and to what degree will you allow this process to consume your life?

Decide on a plan B if the above limits are reached with no success. Determine to go with that plan and follow the Lord's lead.

Father, I give you my goal for a child. Please show us what options to pursue and which ones to say "no" to. We need Your wisdom as we set goals and limits for our baby quest. I commit our family into Your hands and look forward to what You have in store for us.

○✝◆✝○

Don't be consumed with the goal. Be consumed with God's goals for you.

What infertility treatments do I believe would have the Lord's blessing?

_____

_____

_____

_____

_____

_____

_____

_____

_____

_____

_____

_____

_____

_____

_____

_____

_____

_____

_____

~ ♦ ~

Day 8 with Nancy

Perseverance

*And not only this, but we also exult in our tribulations,
knowing that tribulation brings about perseverance;
and perseverance, proven character;
and proven character, hope..."*
Romans 5:3–4

Here in the United States, we live in an age when things can be obtained almost immediately. Our instant society has programmed us to be impatient. We are discouraged by long wait times, because we are not used to persevering until a goal is reached.

Trials, like infertility, require perseverance. Often, our perseverance muscles are weak, and we wear down quickly when forced to use them. We want things to be easy, and when we are called upon to persevere, we usually do all we can to resist discomfort and disappointment.

During these trials, well-intentioned friends sometimes offer poor theology that beats us down rather than builds the scaffolding of encouragement. In these moments, we must do two things to fight hopelessness: persist with our hope in God and be determined to not to give up on our heart's desire, unless He tells us otherwise.

A walk through infertility is an exercise in trusting the Lord, working hard, and not giving up. It teaches us the life skill of perseverance that will help us the rest of our lives, including when we become parents.

Thank You, Jesus, for teaching me to persevere through my struggle with infertility. Please forgive me when I've resisted Your working hand. Your Word says that You are developing character within me, and because of this, I can have hope.

∘✝◆✝∘

Perseverance is the art of never giving up.

How can I submit to the work God is doing in my life?

_____

_____

_____

_____

_____

_____

_____

_____

_____

_____

_____

_____

_____

_____

_____

_____

_____

_____

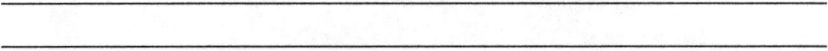

~◆~

Day 9 with Kelly

The Grief in Infertility

Therefore humble yourselves under the mighty handoff
God,
that he may exalt you at the proper time,
casting all your anxiety on him, because He cares for you.
1 Peter 5:6–7

Not long ago, a friend found out she was pregnant. She was so excited, but a few days later started spotting. The doctor told her not to get her hopes up. It was still early in the pregnancy and anything could happen. Her hCG level measured lower than it should, and the doctor arranged for her to have her blood drawn again later that same week.

She was in tears. "How do I deal with this?"

My cheeks dampened, as I wrapped my arms around her and prayed for her and the child.

A few days later, I called to check on her and learned the sad news that she had lost the baby.

"Everyone around me is acting like my loss is no big deal, almost like I don't even have a right to be sad." She stifled a sob. "My neighbor said it's nature's way of terminating defective eggs, and I'm better off now, because who knows what was wrong with them?"

I heard the ache in her voice.

"The nurse at the doctor's office told me not to cry, because it wasn't even a baby yet."

We both knew differently.

Proverbs 18:21 says, "The tongue has the power of life and death" (NIV).

What my friend needed was life spoken to her, not death. I told her a life was lost, and parents should be sad. We need to grieve before we can heal.

For many who deal with infertility, a miscarriage is devastating. Take your grief to the Lord. He understands and does not belittle your loss, for He holds your little one in His hands.

Father, thank you for allowing me to bring my grief and broken heart to You. No one but You fully understands the depth of my sorrow. Please mend my heart so that I can be a soothing balm to others who encounter such losses. Fill my emptiness with hope so that I will not waste my pain but rise above it to bring comfort to others.

∘✝◆✝∘

God is the healer of my heart.

What grief and heartache can I give to the Lord?

_____

_____

_____

_____

_____

_____

_____

_____

~ ◆ ~

Day 10 with Nancy
Taking Steps

The mind of man plans his way,
But the Lord directs his steps
Proverbs 16:9

After I underwent a laparoscopy, my doctor stood at the end of my bed and said he found nothing wrong. "Just relax and keep trying," he told my husband and me. We went home, took a vacation, and kept trying to conceive for another year with no success. In truth, we were doing nothing new to obtain our goal.

Have you been told the same thing by well-meaning friends or your primary care doctor? It is said that attempting something over and over again while expecting a different result is the definition of insanity. I think there's some truth in this old adage. How long have you been *relaxing* and *trying* or using a certain treatment? Is God delaying? Or should you be moving?

If you have tried to conceive for more than a year with what you're doing, I would suggest you prayerfully investigate natural treatments, engage an infertility specialist, or talk to your doctor about trying something different. Yes, the Lord could be delaying, but He also can't lead us if we aren't moving. Is the Lord waiting for you to take another step?

Help me to follow Your leading, Lord, and trust You with my heart's desire. Thank You for Your love and concern. Remind me that You are present in my struggle and will always be by my side.

०✝ ◆ ✝०

I must take the steps as He leads the way.

Is there something I could be doing differently?

_____
_____
_____
_____
_____
_____
_____
_____
_____
_____
_____
_____
_____
_____
_____
_____
_____
_____
_____
_____

Day 11 with Nancy

Natural Treatments?

But if any of you lacks wisdom, let him ask of God,
who gives to all generously and without reproach,
and it will be given to him.
But he must ask in faith without any doubting,
for the one who doubts is like the surf of the sea,
driven and tossed by the wind.
James 1:5–6

If I could accomplish a do-over, I would have been more hesitant to jump on the medical infertility wagon. Our desire for a child can be so strong we don't care what infertility drugs may do to us in the long term. After all I've been through, I've discovered that natural treatments can work wonders and often don't have the negative side effects drugs can have. At the time, I didn't know I had a genetic disease that was made worse because of them.

Pray for wisdom.

Have you considered natural treatments? I'm not a doctor and can't give medical advice, but one of the regrets I have is not investigating natural treatments first. Our bodies are complex and getting one's chemistry right and the body healthy can help tremendously.

Pray for wisdom.

With the Internet and God by our side, we can do a lot of research in a short amount of time. It wouldn't hurt to take a trip to the local health food store, too, and see what they have to offer. This advice comes with a big word of caution. Foods and supplements can have a powerful effect on the body. Be sure to do your research thoroughly.

Pray, pray, pray for wisdom and research, research, research!

Father, please direct my research and give me wisdom as to what to try and what to stay away from. You are the Author of wisdom and have promised to give it to me. Thank You, Lord. You don't expect me to muddle through hard times alone.

∘✝◆✝∘

Seeking the Giver of wisdom is wisdom.

What can I investigate regarding infertility with the Lord at my side?

_____

_____

_____

_____

_____

_____

_____

_____

_____

_____

_____

_____

_____

_____

_____

~ ◆ ~

Day 12 with Kelly
Poly What?

Great is our Lord and abundant in strength;
His understanding is infinite.
Psalm 147:5

Many women dealing with infertility are diagnosed with polycystic ovary syndrome (PCOS). Doctors don't know what causes the disease, only that it can lead to infertility. Studies are now showing a genetic component as well as hormone and insulin links

A woman I know struggled with infertility and was finally diagnosed with PCOS. She had a cyst the size of a grapefruit on one of her ovaries and had to have both the cyst and an ovary removed. I, too, received the diagnoses of PCOS along with endometriosis, which eventually required the removal of both of my ovaries. Looking back, I wonder how much of that could have been controlled by a better understanding of my hormones and insulin.

Scientists are learning more and more each day about infertility. Even if you have PCOS or some other cause for infertility, there are ways to make pregnancy a real possibility. In spite of and since my diagnosis, the Lord allowed me to give birth to two children.

Remember, our Lord is greater than all of this. From biblical times until today, God has opened wombs after long bouts with infertility. Our true source of help is always in God.

Dear Lord, infertility has knocked me off my feet, but don't let me forget that You are greater than any diagnosis. You know every organ and cell in my body. Bring them into alignment with Your design. I am thankful I can take refuge in You.

o✞♦✞o

God is greater than any diagnosis.

What do I believe is greater than God?

_____

_____

_____

_____

_____

_____

_____

_____

_____

_____

_____

_____

_____

_____

_____

_____

_____

_____

_____

_____

_____

_____

_____

~♦~

Day 13 with Nancy

We Are in This Together

See to it that no one comes short of the grace of God;
that no root of bitterness springing up causes trouble,
and by it many be defiled.
Hebrews 12:15

In the year 1536, Anne Boleyn, the second wife of England's Henry VIII, lost her head due to trumped up charges of adultery. Henry, desperate for a male heir, took extreme measures in pursuit of this obsession. To the king's dismay, Anne Boleyn produced only a daughter. She had at least two more pregnancies, which ended in miscarriage or stillbirth. One child, history reports, may have been a boy.

The king blamed his wives for failing to produce a male heir, but today we know through modern science the culprit was none other than the king himself. The male sperm determines the sex of the child. For years, many believed a defect in the woman caused infertility, but we now know that the problem cuts both ways. The husband may have a low sperm count, slow-moving sperm, or some other issue.

Regardless of the cause of a couple's infertility, the quest for a child should not take precedence over the relationship with your spouse. If it has, the yearning has turned to an obsession. A desire, unchecked, will turn anyone into an unhappy, bitter, and possibly conniving person.

Give the situation to the Lord, and pray for love and grace for your spouse. Determine not to sink into bitterness if your spouse happens to be the issue. When you married, you became one. You are in this together. No longer is this a his or her problem. We must always think of infertility as "our struggle".

Help me, Lord, not to become bitter through our struggle with infertility. Please give me Your grace to walk through this valley in a way that will honor my spouse, and most of all, honor You.

∘✝◆✝∘

We are in this together with Jesus.

Who may I be blaming for my situation? How can I open the door of forgiveness and set them free?

_____

_____

_____

_____

_____

_____

_____

_____

_____

_____

_____

~ ◆ ~

Day 14 with Nancy

Tame the Beast

Be of sober spirit, be on the alert.
your adversary, the devil, prowls around like a roaring lion,
seeking someone to devour. But resist him, firm in your faith,
knowing that the same experiences of suffering
are being accomplished by your brethren who are in the world.
1 Peter 5:8–9

Infertility can put a strain on your marriage. Medical infertility treatments alone place unnatural demands upon your marital relationship. The bond you have with your spouse is the most important human relationship you'll ever have. Even if you eventually have children, they will grow up and move out into their adult lives. You and your spouse will be left alone once again. Don't allow the struggle with infertility to destroy what you already have. If allowed, the baby quest can become a vicious cycle consuming your life. The enemy of our souls wants to see that happen.

Tame the beast.

Pray with your spouse against the enemy's plan for your marriage, and prayerfully set limits to your quest. The Lord will guide you through this trial. Close the door for Satan to add money woes to your trials. How much money are you willing to spend on treatments? How many cycles will you continue to try? If there is no success within those limits, accept that God is guiding you into something different, possibly adoption.

Once your plan is made, set your life on that course. The enemy would love to snag you into an endless cycle to devour your time, money, and your option to adopt.

Take control. Tame the beast.

Lord, guide our quest for a child and build a hedge of protection around us against the enemy. Please don't allow us to be destroyed and devoured by this trial. Thank You, Father, that You are our protector.

o✝♦✝o

A plan made with God is a plan that succeeds.

What can I do to prevent the enemy from using this trial to destroy my marriage?

_____

_____

_____

_____

_____

_____

_____

_____

_____

_____

_____

_____

~◆~

When Everyone Else Is Pregnant

A soothing tongue is a tree of life,
but perversion in it crushes the spirit.
Proverbs 15:4

Why does it seem, when you want to get pregnant and can't, suddenly everyone around you is pregnant? I remember when I had just taken my umpteenth pregnancy test with another negative result, a good friend told me she was pregnant again and hadn't even tried.

It's hard to be happy for someone who has kids and is pregnant once again when all you want in the world is to have at least one child. I took so many pregnancy tests that I should have bought stock in the company. My friends and co-workers told me not to lose faith and to keep positive, and each time I followed their advice, my outlook brightened. Each negative test after that wasn't as bad when I remembered that positive words bring life and negative words bring death.

While you are going through infertility, find the positive and grab onto it with both hands. If you know others going through this struggle, encourage them to do the same.

Lord, help me to speak positive words when it seems like pregnancy comes easy for other women but not for me. Father, help me to trust in Your timing and to keep my thoughts positive.

○✝◆✝○

God turns bad situations around for good. So look up.

What positive things have come from infertility in my life? What lessons have I learned?

_____
_____
_____
_____
_____
_____
_____
_____
_____
_____
_____
_____
_____
_____
_____
_____
_____
_____
_____
_____
_____
_____
_____
_____

~ ◆ ~

Is Having a Baby Impossible?

"For nothing will be impossible with God."
Luke 1:37

It might surprise you that this famous verse was given in the context of infertility. In the first chapter of Luke, Zacharias served as a priest in the Jewish Temple. His wife, Elizabeth, was barren, and they both were up in years. One day, as Zacharias performed his priestly duties, the angel Gabriel appeared to him and announced his wife would become pregnant.

Months later, Gabriel appeared to Mary and told her that she would become pregnant and give birth to the Messiah, Jesus. Gabriel then said, "And behold, even your relative Elizabeth has also conceived a son in her old age; and she who was called barren is now in her sixth month. "For nothing will be impossible with God." (Luke 1:36-37).

Have you received a report from your doctor that explains why you haven't gotten pregnant? Have you started your period again? Have you recently miscarried? The story about Zacharias and Elizabeth proves that the Lord cares about the barren woman. Elizabeth is mentioned when the most pivotal event in the history of the entire universe is about to happen, the birth of the foretold Jewish Messiah, Jesus.

Hold on to this verse and keep it buried in your heart.

Thank You so very much, Father, that You are mindful of the barren woman. You see my pain, hear my prayers, and perform miracles. Please help me wait expectantly for the miracle You will work in my life.

○✝◆✝○

Our miracle-working God is mindful of us.

How does the above story pertain to me?

_____

_____

_____

_____

_____

_____

_____

_____

_____

_____

_____

_____

_____

_____

_____

_____

~ ◆ ~

Day 17 with Nancy

Are You Trusting in Him?

On God my salvation and my glory rest;
The rock of my strength, my refuge is in God.
***Trust in Him at all times,** O people;*
Pour your heart out before Him;
God is a refuge for us.
Psalm 62:7–8 (emphasis added)

Are we waiting in silence for God, or are we complaining that He does not hear us and answer our prayers quick enough? Does our glory rest on Him, or on our finances or health insurance? Are we truly trusting Him through this time of infertility? The trial of infertility often challenges our faith and trust in God. We wonder if He has forgotten us and think we've been overlooked. I can assure you this is not the case.

What is trusting God? It's letting go of our wants and needs and receiving His will. In Psalm 46:10, the Lord tells us to *"cease striving and know that I am God."* Is the Lord *God* of our situations, or are we striving in our own strength to make our dream of parenthood come true?

We need to keep our faith strong and trust in the Lord. He knows what He's doing. He may be planning something special for our families. The Bible gives at least six instances where infertility played into God's purposes. As we trust Him, we will learn lessons that will be a goldmine throughout the rest of our lives.

Dear Father, am I truly trusting You with the building of my family? Show me how to trust You in a way that pleases You.

∘✝◆✝∘

Trust is putting the Lord at the controls of our life and allowing Him to take us where He wills.

In what circumstance can I trust the Lord more?

_____

_____

_____

_____

_____

_____

_____

_____

_____

_____

_____

_____

_____

_____

_____

_____

_____

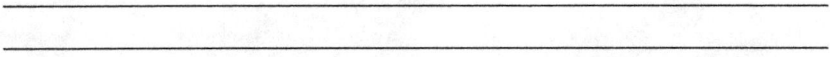

Day 18 with Kelly

An Amazing Gift

As each one has received a special gift,
Employ it in serving one another as good stewards
of the manifold grace of God.
1 Peter 4:10

Alfred Nobel was a very smart man in several areas: math, chemistry, and biology, to name a few. In his early years, he made a name for himself when he invented dynamite. Some years later in his life, a local paper misreported his death, and he had the privilege of reading his obituary.

This experience had a profound effect on Alfred as he realized his life was best remembered as an inventor of destruction. From that moment on, he set out with a new purpose to change the world for the better. Today, he is best known as the founder of the Nobel Peace Prize.

We must be careful to not allow infertility to define us or hold us back from making our lives count. We might not be an Alfred Nobel, but we still can make a positive impact on the world by the strength of our character, in our teaching, in our words, and by our actions. God has given each of us special gifts, and when we use them for His glory, the strength of our characters shine brightly.

At times, we may feel isolated in our struggle with infertility, but we still can turn our focus outward and give encouragement or a helping hand to another. We are stronger than we think.

Lord, what an amazing gift You gave Alfred Nobel, to see what he would be remembered for and then change it. Not all of us are given that opportunity, but Father, I pray that I live my life with purpose and encouragement to others. Help me to see the areas I need to work on and open my heart to a willingness to change.

∘✝◆✝∘

Use your God-given gifts, for in them lies your destiny.

If I died today, what would people remember me for?

_____

_____

_____

_____

_____

_____

_____

_____

_____

_____

_____

_____

_____

_____

_____

_____

_____

_____

_____

_____

~ ◆ ~

The Value of Patience

I waited patiently for the Lord;
And He inclined to me and heard my cry.
He brought me up out of the pit of destruction,
out of the miry clay,
And He set my feet upon a rock making my footsteps firm.
Psalm 40:1–2

If you're like me, the word *patience* makes your skin crawl. In today's instant society, we don't want to wait for anything. We desire to check off our "to do" list as soon as possible and move on to something else.

Waiting to have a child was not in our plans. We assumed we would conceive as soon as we decided the time was right to have a child. This assumption came from the erroneous belief that we were in control. The Lord used this delay to adjust our thinking and prepare us for our eventual jobs as parents. He was the one in control, and we were deluded to think otherwise.

Like the above scripture, He brought my husband and me up out of the muddy pit of wrong thinking, impatience, pride, and selfishness; cleaned us up; and set our feet on the firm ground of knowing Him more fully. He put a new song of praise in our hearts as we've seen Him work miracles. We trust Him more because of them. Others trust Him more because of what they have seen Him do in our lives.

His thoughts are good toward us. Trust Him and wait patiently. He is doing something special in your life. A patient parent is a prepared parent.

I believe Your thoughts are good toward me, Lord. Please forgive my impatience. Help me to trust You as You work in my life to prepare me for the days ahead. Thank You, Jesus.

∘✝◆✝∘

In the soil of patience, flowers of character grow.

In what areas in my life do I need to wait patiently for the Lord's timing?

_____

_____

_____

_____

_____

_____

_____

_____

_____

_____

_____

_____

_____

_____

_____

~ ◆ ~

Day 20 with Nancy

Thankfulness Calms The Heart

You have turned for me mourning into dancing;
You have loosed my sackcloth and girded me with gladness,
That my soul may sing praise to You and not be silent.
O Lord my God, I will give thanks to You forever.
Psalm 30:11–12

Take stock of all the good things God has given you. The desire for a child can be intense, and on this journey, we can sometimes become blinded to His gifts. Taking time every day to thank the Lord for all the wonderful things He has done in our lives can be a salve on our weary hearts. This exercise will refocus our perspectives and allow us to realize we have much to be thankful for. For starters, we have spouses who love us and the Lord who walks by our side.

God loves a grateful heart.

If we cultivate gratitude in our relationships with God and others, the effort will change our outlook on life, which will then alter our world.

Open my eyes, Father, to all the blessings You have given me. Please forgive me for not noticing the blessings of Your hand. Thank You for meeting all my needs and for hearing my prayers. Thank You for being a loving God, who is mindful of me and the trials I face.

o✝◆✝o

Flowers of joy, peace, and contentment bloom where a grateful heart grows.

Make a list of all the blessings the Lord has given you in the past and present.

_____

_____

_____

_____

_____

_____

_____

_____

_____

_____

_____

_____

_____

_____

_____

_____

_____

_____

_____

Day 21 with Kelly

Who Is Your God?

You shall have no other gods before Me.
You shall not make for yourself an idol,
or any likeness of what is in heaven above or on the
earth beneath or in the water under the earth.
Exodus 20:3–4

I know the disappointment of taking pregnancy test after pregnancy test all with negative results. We often take infertility as a sign of punishment for what we have done wrong. It's a conundrum why some women get pregnant at the drop of a hat and others struggle for years. My sister-in-law and my brother simply need to think about trying for a child and she gets pregnant. Three times on the first try.

We tried and tried and tried, and still nothing. I visited doctor after doctor. They put me on Clomid. Still nothing, except weight gain! Finally, when I was at my lowest point, I asked God why He wasn't blessing us with a child. The answer didn't come right away, but when it did, I realized I had made having a child my god.

When I surrendered and got on my knees in prayer, I repented of the little god in my life. I told the Lord He was my God, and if I never got pregnant, He would still be number one. It took a lot of courage to say that. I knew it had to be sincere. Letting go of something I had held on to for so long wasn't easy. I wept for more than an hour, but it was freeing. The chains of failure that had kept me captive were of my own making, and when I set them at the feet of Jesus, I was free again.

Not long after that pivotal moment, I learned I was pregnant. When we let other things become greater than God, failure comes. He doesn't like to share us with false gods, because they will bring us nothing except heartache and death.

Lord, show me if I have any other gods before You in my life. Father, I want to serve only You. Forgive me if I have placed other priorities above You. In You and You alone, I place my hope.

∘✝◆✝∘

Surrender all to Jesus.

Am I serving other gods? What do I need to surrender to the living and true God?

_____

_____

_____

_____

_____

_____

_____

_____

_____

_____

_____

_____

_____

_____

_____

_____

~ ◆ ~

Day 22 with Nancy

Where The Road Leads

But the path of the righteous is like the light of dawn,
That shines brighter and brighter until the full day.
Proverbs 4:18

O ne of the hard things about infertility is it exposes us to ourselves. Emotions become raw, and all our insecurities bubble to the surface. We wonder secretly if we have become second-class citizens to the human race.

We face a road we don't want to walk. We may recognize that our loving Heavenly Father is leading us, but at the same time, we admit to ourselves that we are reluctant followers.

Are we willing to follow the Lord on this road of infertility? Are we ready to lay down our dreams and follow Him into the future? We can choose to either kick, scream, and fight as we journey down this road, or we can accept the road He has us on.

If we give in and walk with faith on the path He has set before us, the darkness of our struggle will give way to the light of dawn, and as the above scripture promises, our path will shine brighter and brighter.

I must admit, Father, I don't want to walk the road You've set before me, but I believe You have my best in mind. Help me not to resist what is ahead. Thank You for Your leading and care.

○†◆†○

Where the path is dark, narrow, and steep, He will light our every step.

What can I do to follow the road the Lord has me travelling on?

_____
_____
_____
_____
_____
_____
_____
_____
_____
_____
_____
_____
_____
_____
_____
_____
_____
_____
_____
_____
_____
_____
_____
_____
_____
_____
_____
_____
_____
_____
_____

~ ♦ ~

Day 23 with Nancy

Choosing to
Remain Childless

Faithful is He who calls you,
and He also will bring it to pass.
1 Thessalonians 5:24

Over coffee, I had a conversation with two middle-aged friends. With hesitancy, one friend admitted she had no children. My other friend then confessed she had never given birth either. I had always wondered if these two women had children, but I never asked because I sensed this was a sensitive topic. They both shared how they felt judged by some Christians, because they'd not been "fruitful and multiplied".

This saddened me.

God has not called us all to standard lives. Just as some are called to be single, some are called to be childless. Not all are called to adopt or to give birth. Yes, there are those who choose not to have children for selfish reasons, but it should never be assumed.

If there is not an insatiable desire to have a child, no matter what the cost, then perhaps you've been called to remain childless. This calling is as valuable as any other. A childless couple is more available for God's service.

The Lord knows your future. My husband and I have friends who went through infertility treatments without success. They then moved toward adoption but didn't have peace about it. A few years later, they discovered they both had medical situations that would make raising children very difficult. They had followed God's lead and made the right decision.

Follow the call of the Lord, and He will bring it to pass.

Am I following Your call, Lord, or the call of others' expectations? Please show me the motive behind my seeking a child. Is there something You are calling me to that a child would make it more difficult to fulfill? Thank You that I can trust Your leading.

∘✝◆✝∘

When we follow His call, we discover our purpose.

How desperate am I for a child? Could I be content without children?

_____

_____

_____

_____

_____

_____

_____

_____

_____

_____

_____

_____

_____

_____

_____

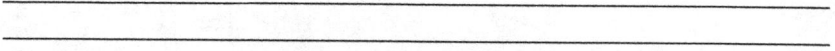

~ ◆ ~

Day 24 with Kelly
Grief Later in Pregnancy

Surely our griefs He Himself bore,
And our sorrows He carried ...
Isaiah 53:4

Grief: a word people use to describe the horrendous emotion that comes after a great loss or death. Words fail to describe the sorrow that comes from the loss of a baby late in pregnancy. For those who have gone through this, my heart breaks for you. Remember, you are not alone. God relates. He sees and hears your pain.

If God knows us in our mother's womb, why does He allow this to happen? For that answer, we must go back to Adam and Eve. When they sinned in the Garden of Eden, the door opened and death invaded our world. Man's rebellion erected a barrier between heaven and earth. Death is a sign of our broken world. God told us if we went our own way, we would suffer death.

God didn't want this for us. But the good news is that when we choose to submit our lives to Him and trust Him with our losses, He uses the heartaches in our lives for good.

Lord, even in my darkest hour, help me to know You are near. I may never understand why this has happened, but Lord I will trust You. In You, I will find rest. Give me courage to face the day, and please give me the peace that surpasses all understanding.

o✝◆✝o

Trusting God with our grief allows Him to bring relief.

How have I given my grief over any loss to the Lord?

_____
_____
_____
_____
_____
_____
_____
_____
_____
_____
_____
_____
_____
_____
_____
_____
_____
_____

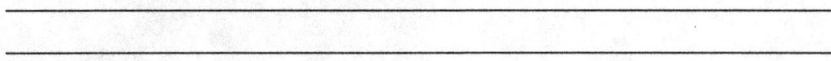

~ ◆ ~

Day 25 with Nancy

Slaying The Spontaneity Killer

I am my beloved's, And his desire is for me.
Come, my beloved, let us go out into the country,
Let us spend the night in the villages.
Let us rise early and go to the vineyards; Let us see whether the
vine has budded
And its blossoms have opened,
And whether the pomegranates have bloomed.
There I will give you my love.
Song of Solomon 7:10–12

Most couples struggling with infertility and undergoing treatment will admit the spontaneity of their love lives has been impacted in a negative way. Many feel as though they are sacrificing a part of their relationship to the fertility god.

Tear down the false god, destroy the idol, and free yourself from its grip. Return to the freedom you and your spouse once had.

As a couple, declare ovulation day to be a special day. Make the occasion fun, sexy, and memorable. Dress up and have a candlelight dinner, or have a picnic at a secluded place in the country. Take a drive down memory lane reliving your dating days, or go out to dinner at a swanky restaurant. If possible, take a one-night, spur-of-the-moment vacation. You get the idea. Be creative. Do silly things.

Focus on fun. Learn to laugh and love again. Even though you've waited a long time for a child, recognize the time you have alone with your spouse is a gift. It's okay to enjoy the gift while you wait for your dream.

Thank You for my spouse, Lord. What a gift You have given me. Help me to focus my energy on my marriage. I place the desire and hope for children in Your hands. Thank You that You are in this with us, and we aren't walking alone. I pray that by Your hand our marriage will be strengthened and our love for each other will grow stronger. My help comes from You.

o✞♦✞o

Make ovulation day a romantic and special day.

Make a list of fun ideas to do on ovulation day.

_____

_____

_____

_____

_____

_____

_____

_____

_____

_____

_____

_____

~ ◆ ~

Day 26 with Kelly

Taking God
Out of The Picture

For the Lord gives wisdom;
From his mouth come knowledge and understanding.
He stores up sound wisdom for the upright;
He is a shield to those who walk in integrity,
Guarding the paths of justice,
And He preserves the way of His godly ones.
Proverbs 2:6–8

Modern science has made many advances on ways to overcome infertility. One of the more controversial methods, particularly in the Christian community, is in vitro fertilization (IVF). Christians believe life begins at conception, and IVF requires several eggs to be fertilized and kept frozen in case the procedure fails. IVF's success rate is at twenty-five percent, about the same as "natural" conception. Many in the Christian community are concerned about the remaining frozen embryos, which are kept in storage and may later be disposed. They see little difference between the disposal of these embryos and abortion.

This issue has directly affected my family. I have a niece and a nephew who were conceived through IVF. It was in the Lord's hands though if they would survive. There are alternatives to IVF and options for use of the frozen embryos stored for IVF. Specifically, other infertility treatments are available that involve eggs being stored without fertilizing them. For instance, Oocyte Cryopreservation is a process in which women can freeze their unfertilized egg indefinitely. For the frozen embryos stored as part of IVF, a program called "Snowflake Babies" gives couples the option of receiving the fertilized eggs to use for their attempts at parenthood.

As technology advances, the limits are expanding on what science is able to do. It can be easy to get caught up in our desires and lose sight of what God wants for us. Daily prayer will help you tread through those uncharted waters.

"Lord, I am fearfully and wonderfully made. You know every part of me, and every thought, and every hair on my head. Without You, Father, I wouldn't be here. For that I give you praise. Help me to always remember that You are the grand designer.

o✟◆✟o

Having knowledge to do something doesn't mean it's wise to do it.

What limits am I willing to place on infertility treatments and then trust God with the rest?

_____

_____

_____

_____

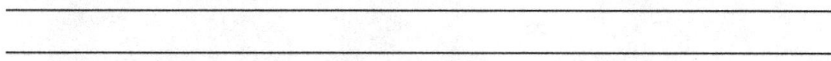

~◆~

Day 27 with Nancy

Struggle Well

Blessed is a man who perseveres under trial;
for once he has been approved,
he will receive the crown of life
which the Lord has promised to those who love Him.
James 1:12

Infertility is an emotional and physical path of struggle for most. The trial can cause doubt and resentment toward the Lord. Some even become mad at God. Envy can occupy our minds toward those who are pregnant or who have large families. Self-doubt creeps in and makes itself at home. We wonder what we've done wrong to be fighting such a battle. All these feelings and questions are normal, but what are we to do?

Determine to struggle well.

Realize there is eternal benefit in our troubles if we choose to learn from them. God doesn't cause difficulties in our lives, but when they come to us, He uses them to make us better people and more like Him.

With every obstacle we face, we are given a choice to either become better or worse. To struggle well, we must trust God and refuse to become resentful. Choosing joyfulness over envy, in spite of our emotions, sets those around us at ease and prevents others from avoiding us.

Some may view acting happy when one is not as dishonest, but emotions come and go. Let's not use our trials as excuses to rain on someone else's parade. We will be better people if we focus on others in spite of our troubles. No one likes a person who is resentful, envious, and has a chip on her shoulder. Put to use this opportunity to become a better person. God is by your side. Ask for His help, and you will grow.

Sometimes it's difficult to share someone else's happiness, Father, when they already have children and I have none. Please give me the strength to honor You in those times. Give me eyes to focus on others and trust that You will be faithful to bring joy to my heart as well.

o†♦†o

Those who struggle well change their thinking to God-like thoughts.

What practical things can I do to share in other people's joy?

_____

_____

_____

_____

_____

_____

_____

_____

_____

_____

_____

_____

_____

_____

~◆~

Day 28 with Kelly

Toxic Thoughts

But if you have bitter jealousy and selfish ambition in your heart,
do not be arrogant and so lie against the truth.
This wisdom is not that which comes down from above,
but is earthly, natural, demonic.
For where jealousy and selfish ambition exist,
There is disorder and every evil thing.
James 3:14–16

Have you ever looked at a family in line in front of you or maybe glanced at a co-worker's desk and seen pictures of their kids and thought that it's not fair that they get a family and you don't?

The study of Epigenetics is how the chemical reaction in genes is expressed at a cellular level, but what scientist are finding now is that choices become signals that change our brain and bodies and are not dictated by our genes. When we allow those seeds of jealousy and resentment to take root, we can affect our ability to conceive. Our very thoughts can be toxic and can prevent us from getting pregnant. According to Dr. Caroline Leaf and many others, if you change your perception you can change your biology.

The Lord wants only good things for us. When we let go of our jealousy and resentment, those toxins get washed away by the Lord's cleansing, and He plants new seeds grown from His love.

Lord, I give You all my jealous thoughts. Please forgive me for harboring them. Help me to keep my thoughts on You and Your will for my life. Help me to see the good in those around me and to join into the joy of their blessings.

○✝◆✝○

Weeds of bitterness choke out the flowers of love.

What seeds of jealousy or resentment have I sown?

_____
_____
_____
_____
_____
_____
_____
_____
_____
_____
_____
_____
_____
_____
_____
_____
_____
_____
_____

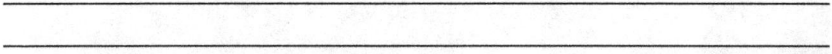

~ ◆ ~

Day 29 with Nancy
Surely You'd Like to Babysit

Whatever you do in word or deed,
do all in the name of the Lord Jesus,
giving thanks through Him to God the Father.
Colossians 3:17

When I struggled with infertility, it seemed some people thought I begged to babysit. Babysitting just increased my pain. I don't know if others thought by letting me babysit, I'd decide I didn't want a child after all, or that I'd make a good "adopted" aunt. I'm not sure of their reasoning, but they probably had not walked in my shoes.

While their requests may seem insensitive to our plight, take a moment to examine their situations. Are they struggling financially or caught in a desperate situation where they really need help? Serving others is a great way to get our minds off our own struggles, and it's an opportunity to serve the Lord.

While I'm not suggesting you allow yourself to be taken advantage of, serving others has its benefits. If we take the attitude that all our service is unto the Lord, it will help eliminate resentful feelings. Remember, if one has not been down the road, they won't know what's on it.

Help me, Jesus, not to take offense when others seem to be insensitive to my struggle. Give me grace to forgive them, knowing they have not experienced the things I have. Show me where I've been guilty of not understanding the trials of others, and help me see the needs of people so I can serve You by serving them.

○✝◆✝○

We serve God when we serve others.

Who can I minister to or serve?

_____
_____
_____
_____
_____
_____
_____
_____
_____
_____
_____
_____
_____
_____
_____
_____
_____
_____
_____
_____

~◆~

Day 30 with Kelly

Angry with God?

Cease from anger and forsake wrath;
Do not fret; it leads only to evildoing.
For evildoers will be cut off,
But those who wait for the Lord, they will inherit the land."
Psalms 37:8–9

Is it all right to be angry with God when things don't go the way we planned? In the book of Psalms, we find a collection of prayers in which the writers show a variety of human emotions from anger to acceptance, despair to happiness, sadness to joy, and more.

Anger at God shows a wrong concept of Him. We live in a broken world because man sinned. The Lord wants a personal relationship with each one of us, and He knows us better than anyone. God created us in His own image. He is patient with us, even when we're angry and don't understand His plans.

Let go of your anger.

Jesus said in this life we would have trouble, but how we deal with difficult things reveals our character. Trials don't *make* us who we are; they *reveal* who we are. God can turn every trial to good if we let Him. We need to work out our doubt and misgivings about Him and believe we will be happy with His purpose for our lives. He truly loves us and wants what is best for us.

God allows our suffering and uses trials to teach us and shape us. Trials bless us with maturity, steadfastness, character, and wisdom.

Thank You, Lord, for my trials. I know You are teaching me and shaping me into who You want me to be. Please give me patience when I don't understand the lesson You are teaching me.

○✝◆✝○

A misunderstanding of God breeds ire toward Him.

What trials am I going through right now? Am I angry at God for these trials? How can I seek truth about who God is?

_____

_____

_____

_____

_____

_____

_____

_____

_____

_____

_____

_____

_____

_____

_____

_____

_____

_____

_____

_____

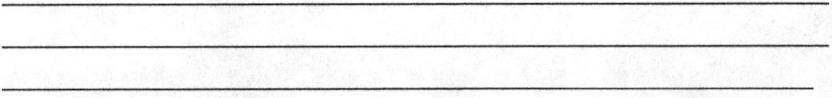

Other Books by These Authors

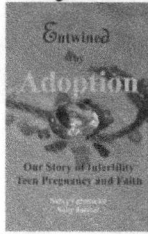

Entwined by Adoption
Our Story of Infertility, Teen Pregnancy and Faith

Adoption is the cord entwined by His design.

PART ONE

Shattered dreams of motherhood lay in Nancy's heart, bludgeoned by infertility. Would she ever feel whole?

The darkness of teen pregnancy engulfed Kelly, swallowing her into the pit of hopelessness. Pregnant? She couldn't be. Her family might disown her.

Could these two women hold the answer to each other's prayers? In this heart wrenching and miraculous, true story of adoption, Kelly and Nancy team up to share how God mends hearts to see the light again.

This book delivers far more than just their story. They present two study journals packed full of practical tips, and answers many questions such as:

PART TWO
- Why does God allow infertility?
- Is infertility a punishment?
- What does the Bible say about infertility and adoption?
- Should I adopt?
- Am I ready to adopt?

PART THREE
- I'm pregnant. Now what?
- Is my life ruined?
- As a parent of a pregnant teen, what should I do?

And much, much more . . .

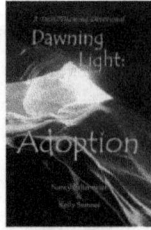

Dawning Light: Adoption

A 30-day Dust2Diamond Devotional is designed to take you on a walk with God. Not only are the spiritual topics of adoption discussed, but the practical as well.

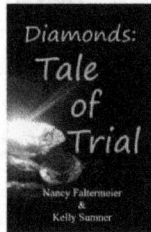

Diamonds: Tale of Trials

Out of the depths of hardship and pain, diamonds rise.

Have you experienced disappointment, rejection, or pain? Do you wonder if you've been forgotten, like no one cares?

Where is God in the midst of our struggles? What good can come from trials?

In this book, we take a look at Joseph's life through the analogy of a gem quality diamond's journey. Beginning as something ugly and black, it turns, through great hardship, into a wondrous beauty that reflects His light in prisms of color.

Visit us at: www.fromdust2diamonds.com

Our Blog: dust2diamonds.wordpress.com

If you have found this book to be helpful, we would love to hear about it. Please write to us at dust2diamonds1@gmail.com. May God bless you on this journey.

ABOUT THE AUTHORS

From Dust2Diamond Authors
Kelly Sumner and Nancy Faltermeier

Kelly Sumner is a teacher with experience in both public and private schools. Her involvement in the teen pregnancy clinic has inspired her to write about her experience as a teenage birth mother. She has published *Broken Dreams Made Whole* in *Apraxia Now* magazine. A magazine devoted to parents of children unable to speak.

She devotes her time to teaching her own preschool, writing fiction for women, young adults, and suspense lovers. Residing in gorgeous Colorado, Kelly lives with her husband, two children, a dog, and a conversational cat. She loves to travel, camp at the lake, and spend time with friends.

Nancy Meyers Faltermeier writes non-fiction and Young Adult fantasy. In past years she worked full time with a ministry noted for the children's albums *Music Machine* and *Bullfrogs and Butterflies.* There she wrote skits, plays, and songs. Music she wrote, found publication in two songbooks and four recordings by different artists.

She has also taught Bible Studies on many different topics and levels. After homeschooling her children through high school, she is dedicating her time bringing hope to the hurting through the written word. Nancy resides at the base of the Rockies in beautiful Colorado with her husband, two adult children, two parakeets, and a backyard nursery of wild cottontail bunnies. In her spare time, she enjoys hiking, amateur photography, and scrapbooking.

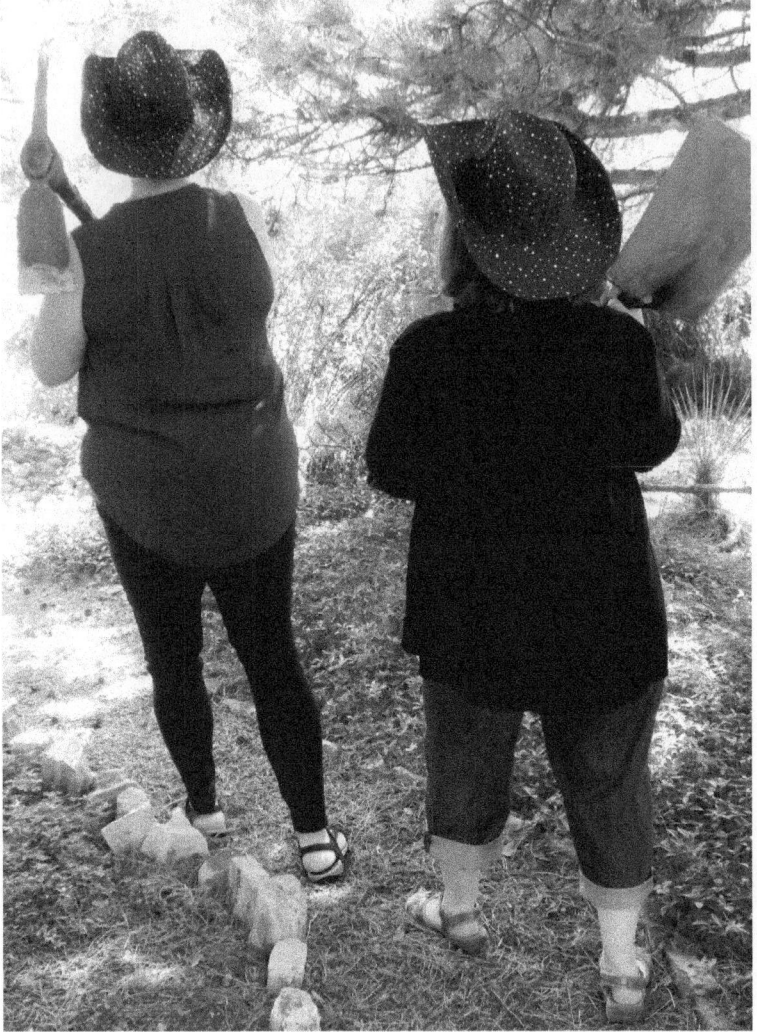

Gone to unearth more truths for hurting hearts.